Camels

Kate Riggs

CREATIVE EDUCATION • CREATIVE PAPERBACKS

seedlings

Published by Creative Education and Creative Paperbacks
P.O. Box 227, Mankato, Minnesota 56002
Creative Education and Creative Paperbacks are
imprints of The Creative Company
www.thecreativecompany.us

Design by Ellen Huber
Production by Chelsey Luther
Printed in the United States of America

Photographs by Dreamstime (Ed Francissen, Eric Gevaert,
Isselee, Katerika, Mahmoud Mahdy, Rumos, Simoly2010),
Getty Images (Martin Harvey, Todd Lawson, Michael S.
Lewis, TARIQ-M), Shutterstock (Iakov Filimonov, Eric
Isselee, panyajampatong, Mariia Savoskula), SuperStock
(imagebroker.net, Norbert Probst/imageb/imagebroker.net,
Stock Connection, Tips Images, Travel Pictures Ltd)

Library of Congress Cataloging-in-Publication Data
Riggs, Kate.
Camels / Kate Riggs.
p. cm. — (Seedlings)
Summary: A kindergarten-level introduction to camels,
covering their growth process, behaviors, the deserts they call
home, and such defining features as their humps.
Includes index.
ISBN 978-1-60818-513-9 (hardcover)
ISBN 978-1-62832-113-5 (pbk)
1. Camels—Juvenile literature. 2. Adaptation (Biology)
—Juvenile literature. I. Title. II. Series: Seedlings.

QL737.U54R544 2015
599.63'62—dc23   2013051256

CCSS: RI.K.1, 2, 3, 4, 5, 6, 7;
RI.1.1, 2, 3, 4, 5, 6, 7; RF.K.1, 3; RF.1.1

First Edition
9 8 7 6 5 4 3 2 1

TABLE OF CONTENTS

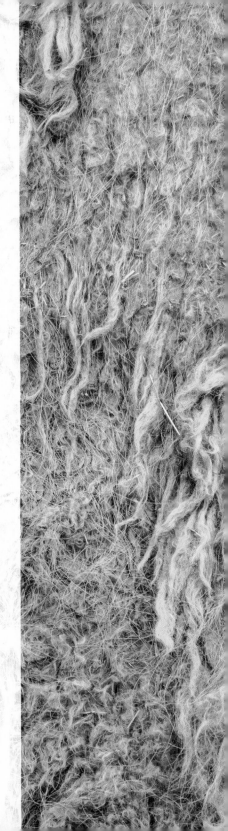

Hello,

camels!

Camels are furry desert animals.

They live in **Asia** and the Middle East.

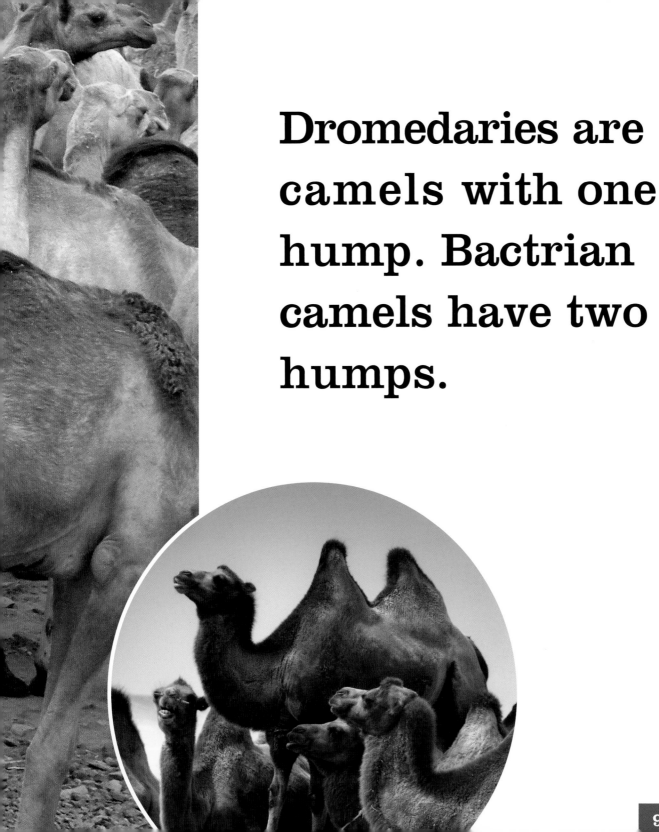

Dromedaries are camels with one hump. Bactrian camels have two humps.

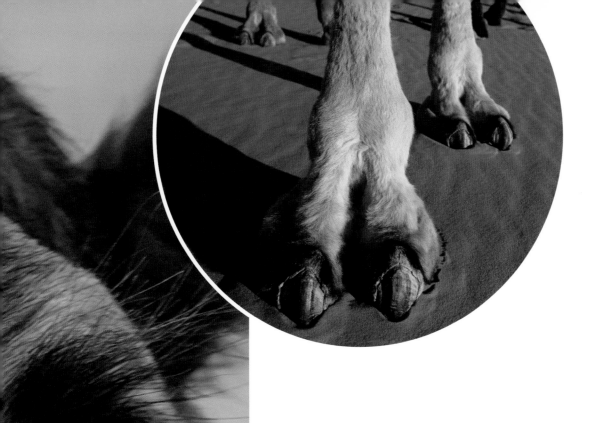

A camel has
thick eyelashes.
It has two toes
on each foot.

Camels eat plants. They grab grasses and other plants with their big teeth.

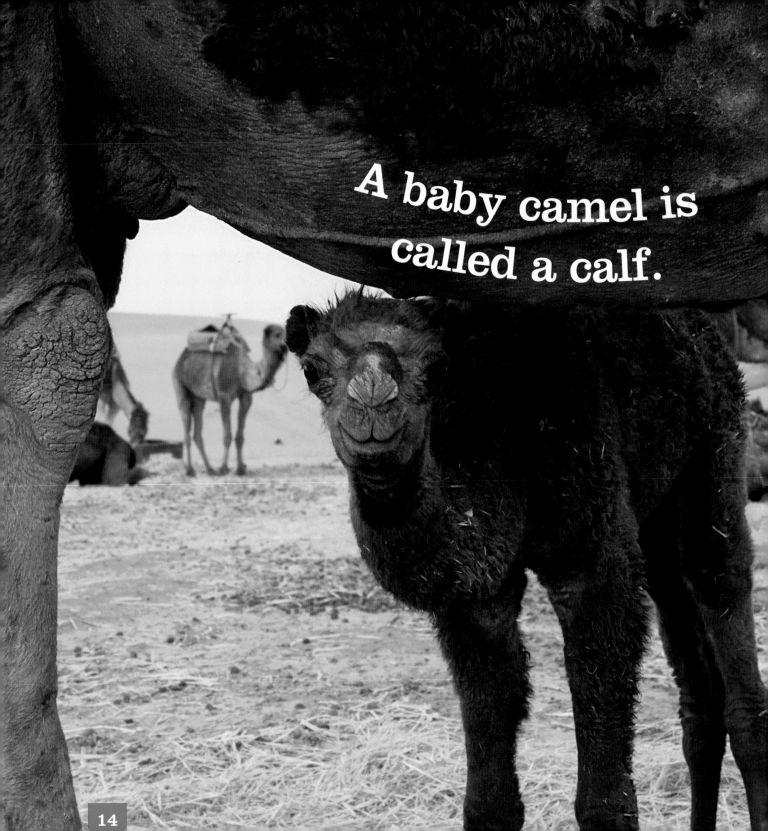

A baby camel is called a calf.

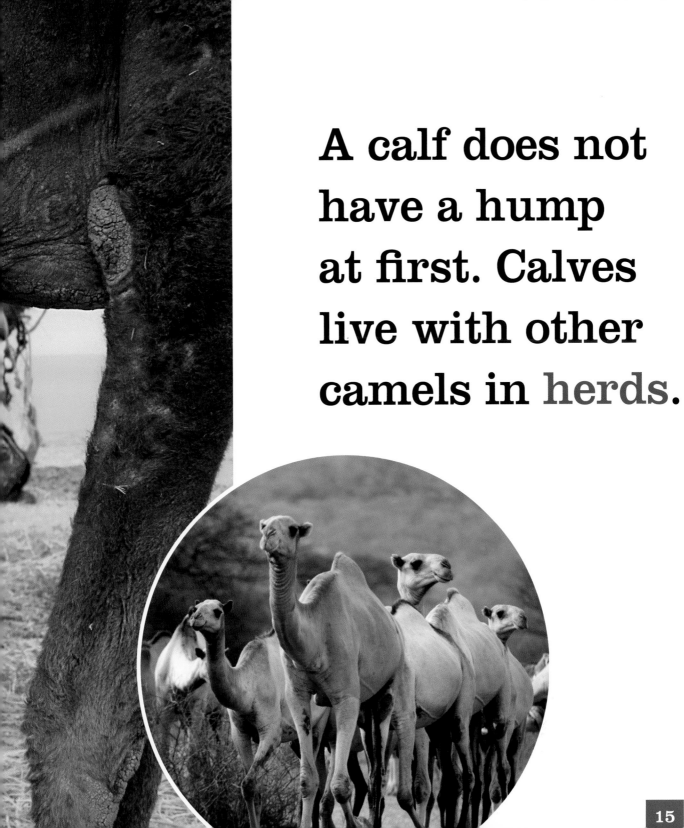

A calf does not
have a hump
at first. Calves
live with other
camels in herds.

Camels walk through the desert. They drink water when they can find it.

Goodbye,

camels!

Picture a Camel

eyelashes

ear

hump

fur

mane

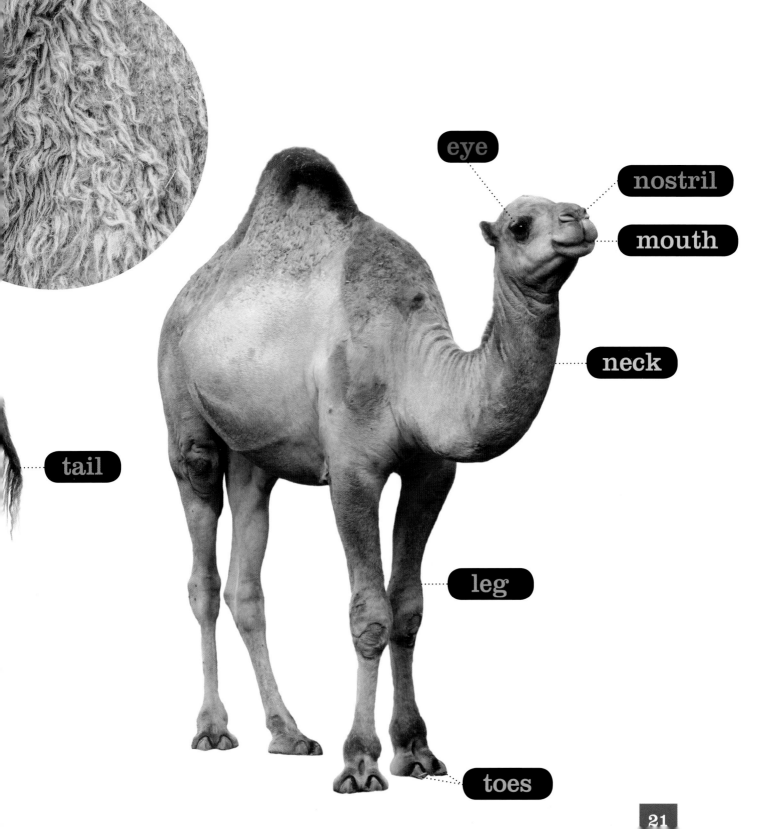

eye

nostril

mouth

neck

tail

leg

toes

Words to Know

Asia: the biggest piece of land in the world

desert: a hot, dry place without much rain

herds: large groups of animals that live together

Middle East: an area of land between Asia and northern Africa

Read More

Borgert-Spaniol, Megan. *Camels*.
Minneapolis: Bellwether Media, 2012.

Ganeri, Anita. *I Wonder Why Camels Have Humps, and Other Questions about Animals*. Boston: Kingfisher, 2003.

Websites

Camel: Find the 10 Differences Game
http://www.hellokids.com/c_24091/free-kids-games/find-the
-differences/animal-difference-games/camel-find-the-10
-differences-game
Color pictures of camels. Find the differences between two
camels that look alike!

Egg Carton Animals
http://www.enchantedlearning.com/crafts/Eggcarton.shtml
Make a camel out of an egg carton and other simple supplies.

Index